Alfred's Basic Piano Library
Chord Approach
A PIANO METHOD FOR THE LATER BEGINNER

Duet Book
LEVEL 1

While this book of duets is correlated with the corresponding level of the Chord Approach to Alfred's Basic Piano Library, teachers should be aware that the pieces are written in a manner which makes them highly adaptable to almost any method. The secondo parts, which can be played by the teacher, parent, or more advanced student, are delightful accompaniments which serve to enhance the student's part. The primo is "complete" in itself, thus creating little solos which become even more fun and motivational when performed as a duet! It is hoped that these duets will bring a smile to the faces of teachers, students, and audiences whether they are performed at the lesson, at home, or on the recital hall stage.

Dennis Alexander

D1279224

DUET PART (Student plays 1 octave higher)

ROCK ALONG WITH ME!

Moderately fast

Use after NOTE READING MADE EASY (page 13)
of Alfred's Basic Chord Approach, Lesson Book 1.

ROCK ALONG WITH ME!

Moderately fast

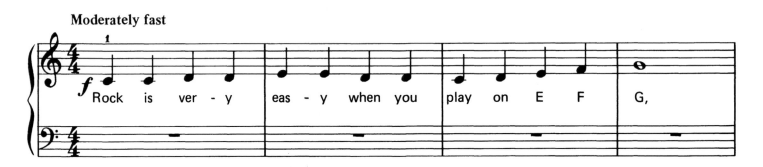

f Rock is ver - y eas - y when you play on E F G,

G G F F E E F now rock a - long with me.

DUET PART (Student plays 1 octave higher)

PICCADILLY WALTZ

Moderately slow

Use after STRANGE LANDS (page 16).

PICCADILLY WALTZ

Moderately slow

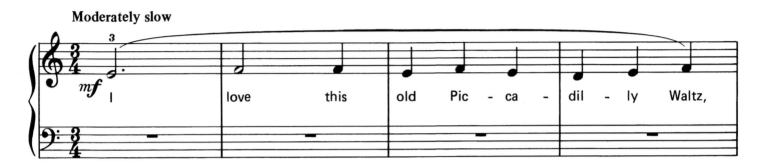

I love this old Pic - ca - dil - ly Waltz,

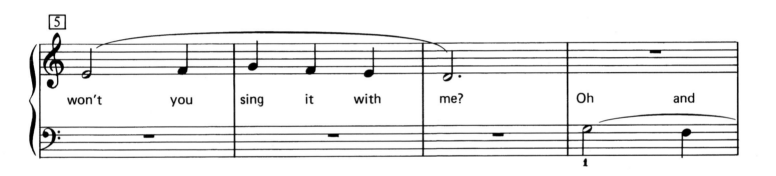

won't you sing it with me? Oh and

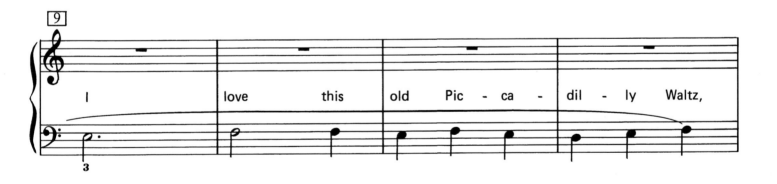

I love this old Pic - ca - dil - ly Waltz,

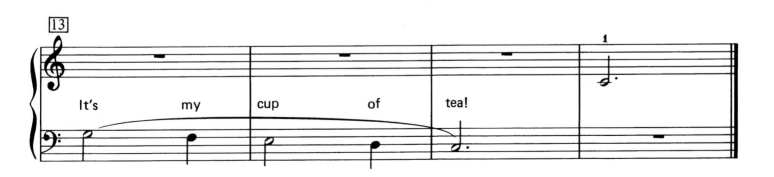

It's my cup of tea!

DUET PART (Student plays 1 octave higher)

DRINK TO ME ONLY

Use after MELODIC FIFTHS (page 23).

DRINK TO ME ONLY

Moderately slow

DUET PART (Student plays 1 octave higher)

SONATINA IN C

Use after JINGLE BELLS (page 24).

SONATINA IN C

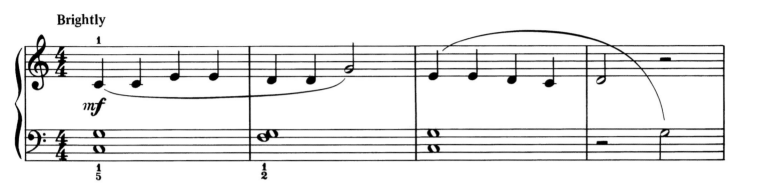

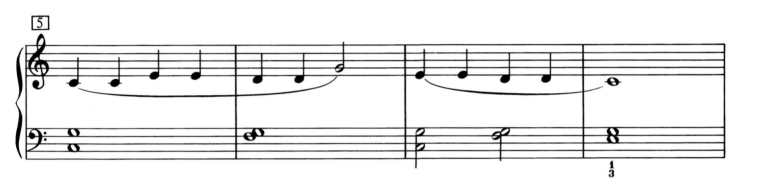

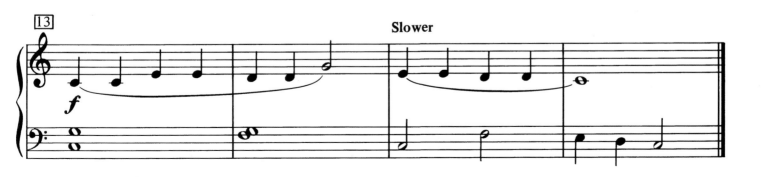

DUET PART (Student plays 1 octave higher)

MUSIC IS LOVE

Use after THE ONE MAN BAND (page 27).

MUSIC IS LOVE

Moderately slow

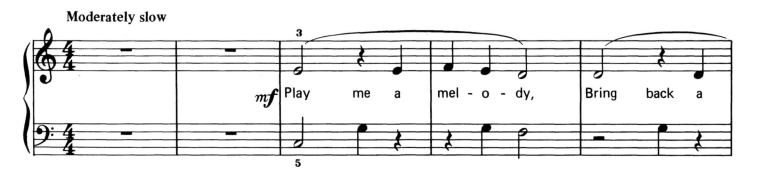

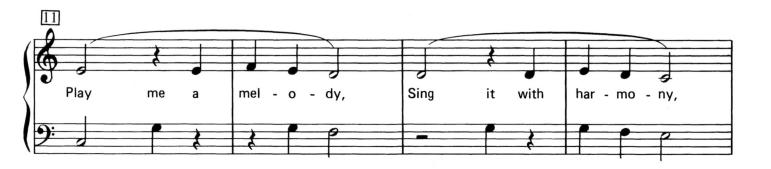

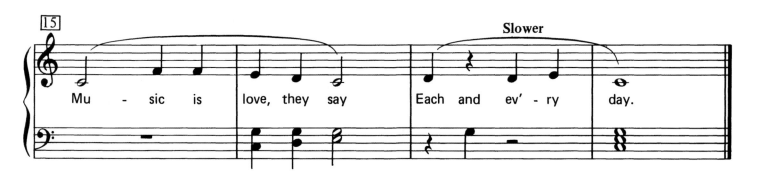

DUET PART (Student plays 1 octave higher)

TWILIGHT MOOD

Use after LARGO (page 29).

TWILIGHT MOOD

DUET PART (Student plays 1 octave higher)

MAYBE TOMORROW

Use after page 36.

MAYBE TOMORROW

DUET PART (Student plays 1 octave higher)

ROCKIN' ROBERTA

With vigor – moderately fast

Use after INTERVALS IN G POSITION (page 38).

ROCKIN' ROBERTA

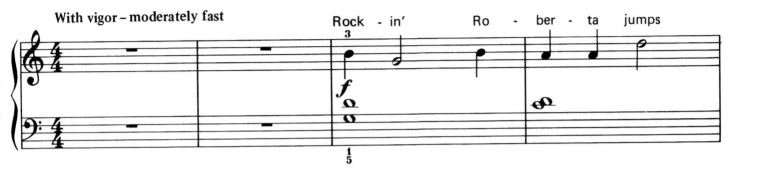

DUET PART (Student plays 1 octave higher)

for Christopher

HOMEWORK BOOGIE

Use after MONEY CAN'T BUY EVERYTHING (page 41).

for Christopher

HOMEWORK BOOGIE

DUET PART (Student plays 1 octave higher)

"A SHARP" WALTZ

Allegro moderato

Use after THE CUCKOO (page 43).

"A SHARP" WALTZ

DUET PART (Student plays 1 octave higher)

BALLAD

Use after THUMBS ON C (page 50).

BALLAD

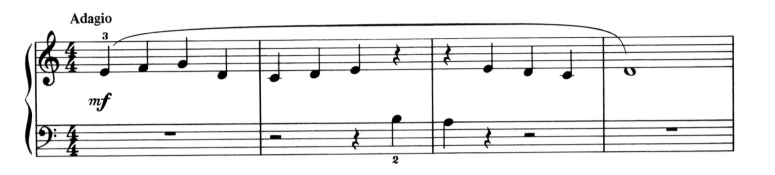

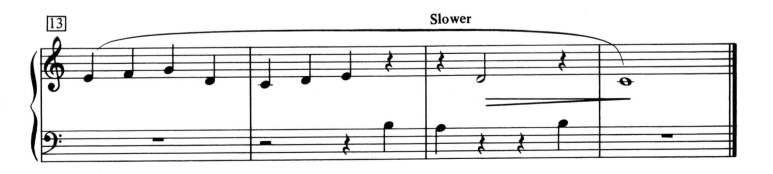

DUET PART (Student plays 1 octave higher)

DAWNING

Use after page 56.

DAWNING

Andante moderato

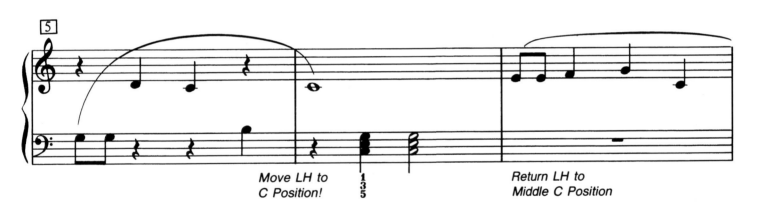

Move LH to
C Position!

Return LH to
Middle C Position

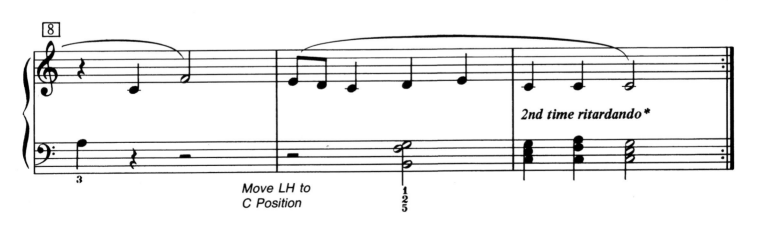

Move LH to
C Position

*2nd time ritardando**

**ritardando* means gradually slowing.*

DUET PART (Student plays 1 octave higher)

CINDY, CINDY

Folk Song

Use after ROCK IT AWAY (page 57).

CINDY, CINDY

Folk Song

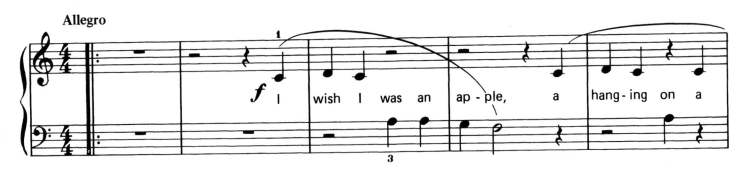

I wish I was an ap - ple, a hang - ing on a

tree, and ev' - ry time my Cin - dy passed she'd take a - bite of me. Get - a - long

home Cin - dy Cin - dy get a - long home Cin - dy, Cin - dy, get a - long

home Cin - dy, Cin - dy, I'll mar - ry you some - day!

 The double dots inside the double bars indicate that
everything between the double bars must be REPEATED.

DUET PART (Student plays 1 octave higher)

CALICO RAG

Use after ROCK IT AWAY (page 57).

CALICO RAG

Allegro moderato

DUET PART (Student plays 1 octave higher)

For Darren
SAXOPHONE ROMP

Use after BOOGIE-WOOGIE GOOSE (page 58).

For Darren

SAXOPHONE ROMP